Let's Learn About...
THE OCEAN
PROJECT BOOK
STEAM

K1

Pearson

Pearson Education Limited
KAO Two, KAO Park, Harlow, Essex, CM17 9NA, England
and Associated Companies around the world

First published 2020
Second impression 2023

ISBN: 978-12-9233-411-0

Set in Mundo Sans
Printed in Slovakia by Neografia

Acknowledgements
The publishers and author(s) would like to thank the following people and institutions for their feedback and comments during the development of the material: Marcos Mendonça, Leandra Dias, Viviane Kirmeliene, Rhiannon Ball, Mônica Bicalho and GB Editorial. The publishers would also like to thank all the teachers who contributed to the development of *Let's learn about...*:
Adriano de Paula Souza, Aline Ramos Teixeira Santo, Aline Vitor Rodrigues Pina Pereira, Ana Paula Gomez Montero, Anna Flávia Feitosa Passos
Camila Jarola, Celiane Junker Silva, Edegar França Junior, Fabiana Reis Yoshio, Fernanda de Souza Thomaz, Luana da Silva, Michael Iacovino Luidvinavicius, Munique Dias de Melo
Priscila Rossatti Duval Ferreira Neves, Sandra Ferito, and schools that took part in Construindo Juntos.

Author Acknowledgements
Luciana Pinheiro and Simara H. Dal'Alba

Image Credit(s):
Shutterstock.com: Macrovector 51

Illustration Acknowledgements
Illustrated by Filipe Laurentino and MRS Editorial

Cover illustration © Filipe Laurentino

CONTENTS

CHOOSE AND COLOR.

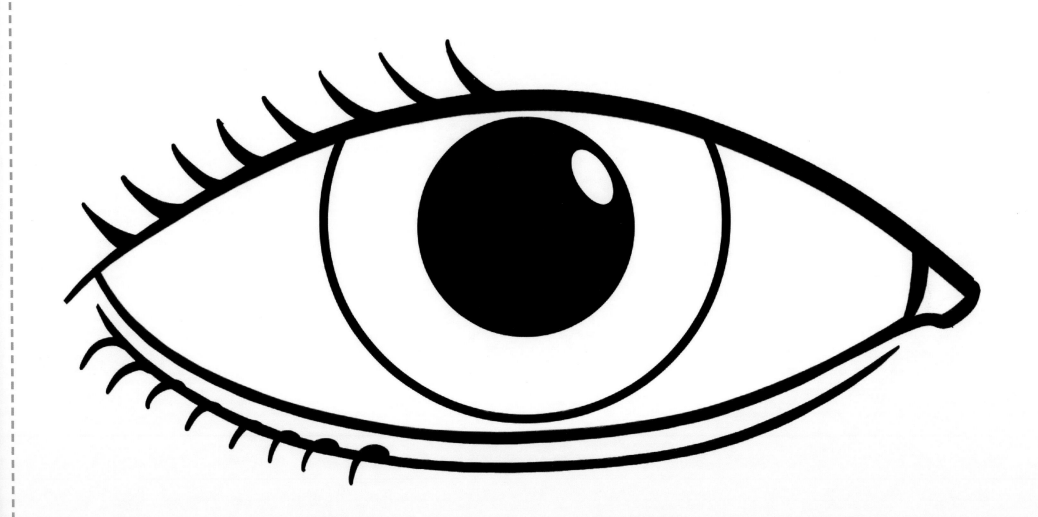

POINT TO YOUR FACE AND COUNT. GLUE.

👁		
👃		
👄		
👂		

COLOR. MAKE A PAIR OF GLASSES.

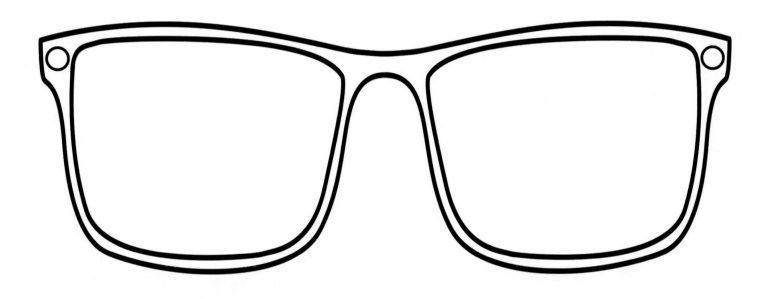

WHICH LIGHT IS MAKING THE SHADOW? CIRCLE.

WHAT DO YOUR CLASSMATES LIKE? DRAW TALLY MARKS.

HOW CAN YOU SHOW WHAT YOUR CLASSMATES LIKE USING BUILDING BLOCKS?

HOW CAN YOU MAKE YOUR DOLL STAND? CIRCLE.

DECORATE YOUR CLASSMATE'S LEG CAST.

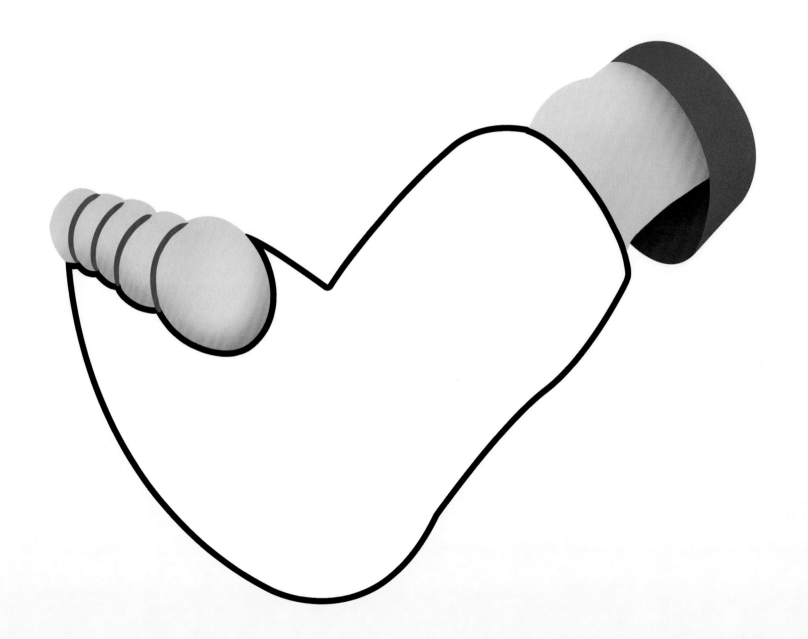

HOW CAN YOU MAKE THE BAR SAFE? GLUE THE STRING TO MAKE A FENCE.

STICK THE ARROWS AND CROSSES TO ORDER THE STORY.

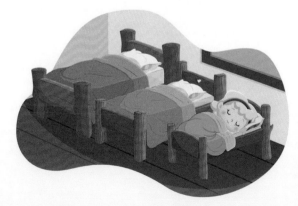

LOOK AND SAY. HOW MANY OF EACH DO YOU NEED FOR THE FAMILY? CIRCLE.

DRAW AND COLOR. GLUE SHUTTERS TO THE HOUSE.

MAKE A COLLAGE TO COLOR DADDY AND BABY UNICORN.

LOOK AND STICK THE TOYS NEXT TO THE SILHOUETTES. 👁 🍐

WHAT CAN YOU USE TO MELT ICE? CIRCLE.

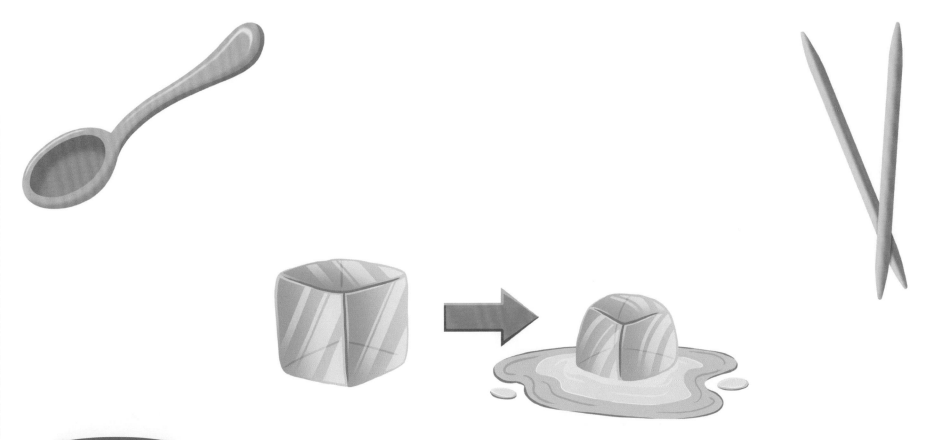

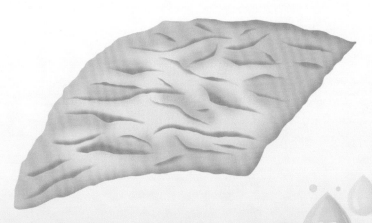

WHICH ROBOT IS ON? WHICH ROBOT IS OFF? COLOR THE POWER BUTTON GREEN OR RED.

MATCH THE BALL WITH THE SLOPE IT ROLLED DOWN.

LOOK AND DRAW A BIG OR A SMALL HOUSE.

WHO CAN DO THESE CHORES? CIRCLE.

WHO SLEEPS IN EACH BED? LOOK AND CIRCLE.

MATCH THE HOUSES WITH THE SHAPES.

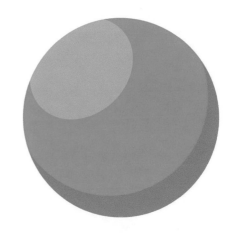

HELP THE SEAHORSE GET BACK TO THE SEA.

WHAT DOES A PET FISH NEED TO LIVE? CIRCLE.

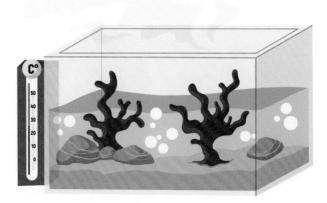

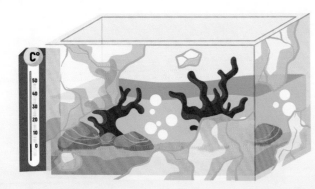

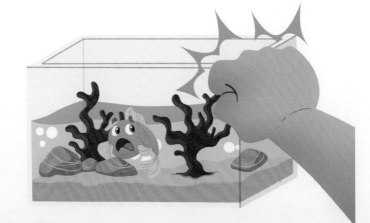

DRAW THE STEPS TO MAKE YOUR PET'S SLEEPING PLACE.

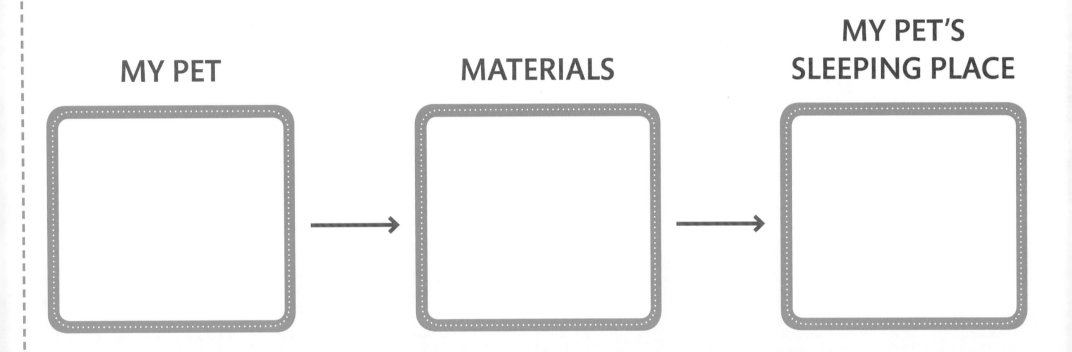

MY PET

MATERIALS

MY PET'S
SLEEPING PLACE

WHICH PETS SLEEP ON A BED? CIRCLE GREEN. WHICH ANIMALS DON'T LIE DOWN TO SLEEP? CIRCLE BLUE.

MAKE A TOPPING FOR YOUR PIZZA SLICE.

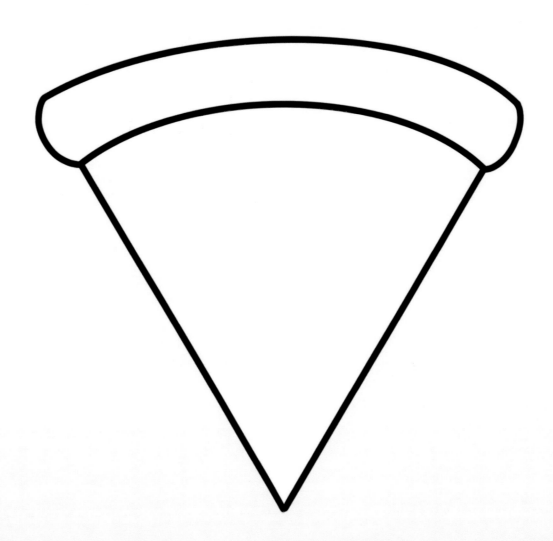

WHICH FRUIT IS THE BUG? STICK. 👁️ 🍐

WHICH PICTURE IS MISSING FROM THE PUZZLE? LOOK AND CIRCLE.

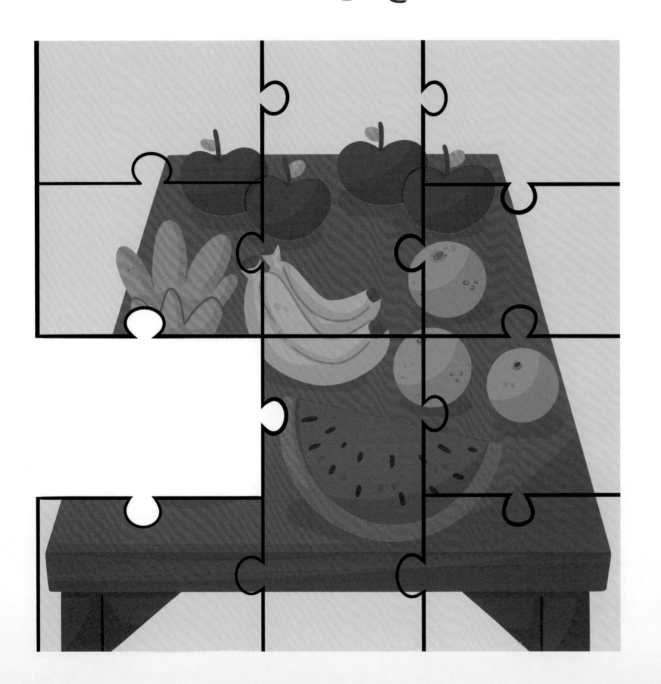

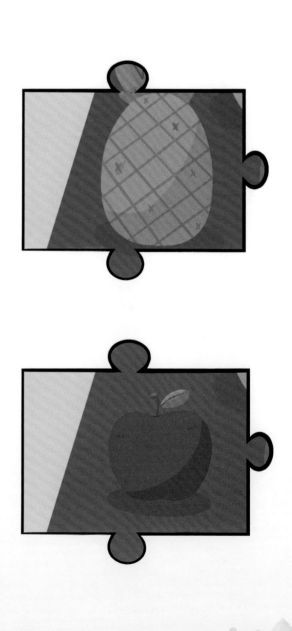

MATCH THE PLASTIC FOOD CONTAINERS WITH THEIR LID.

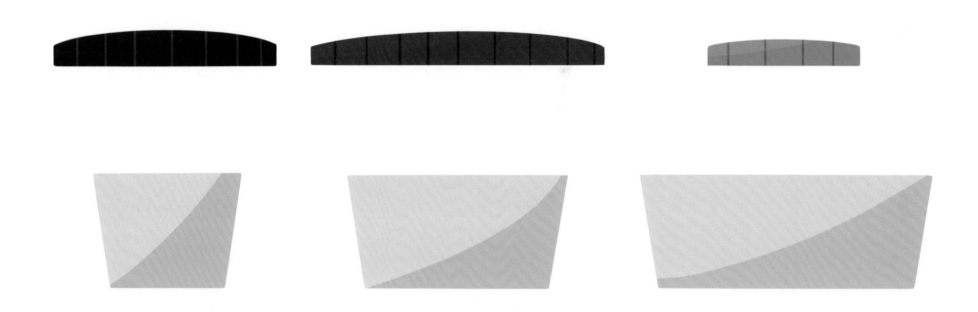

PUT CLAY ON THE SHAPES. CLOSE YOUR EYES, TOUCH, AND SAY. 👄

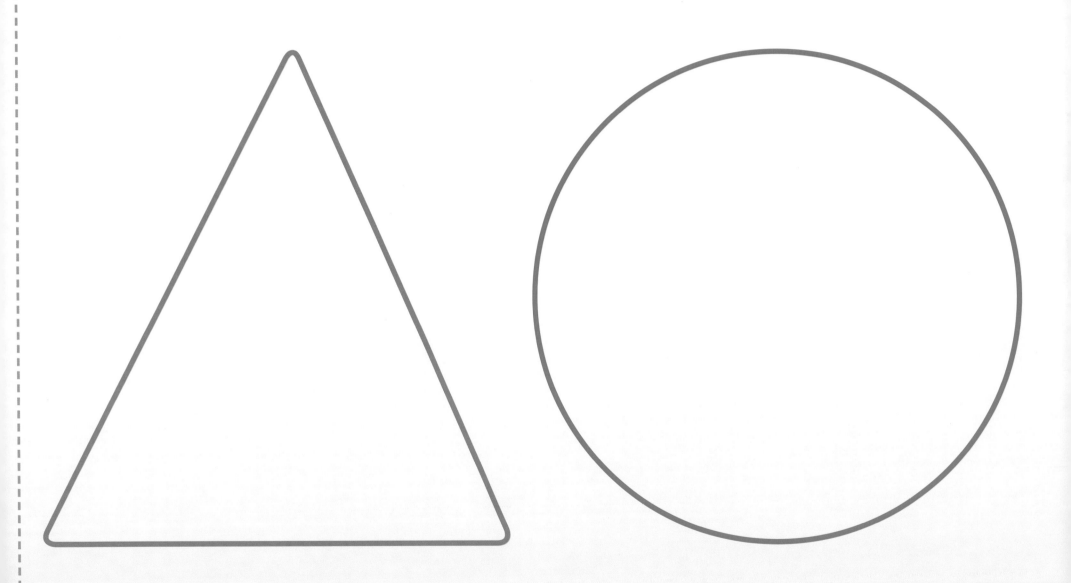

DRAW THE SEQUENCE FOR THE MINDFULNESS ACTIVITY.

WHAT DOES YOUR SCHOOL LOOK LIKE? MAKE A POINTILLIST PAINTING.

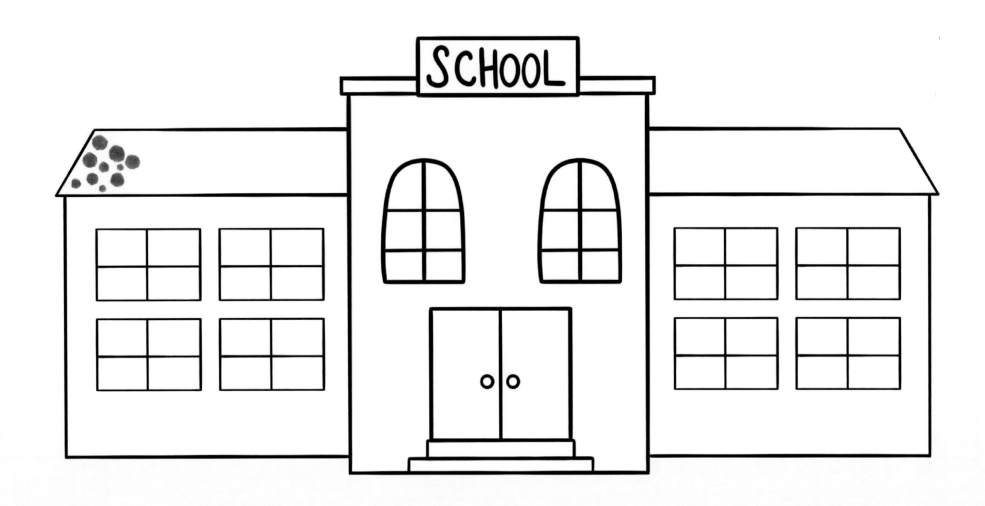

FIND THE BUGS. HOW CAN YOU FIX THEM?

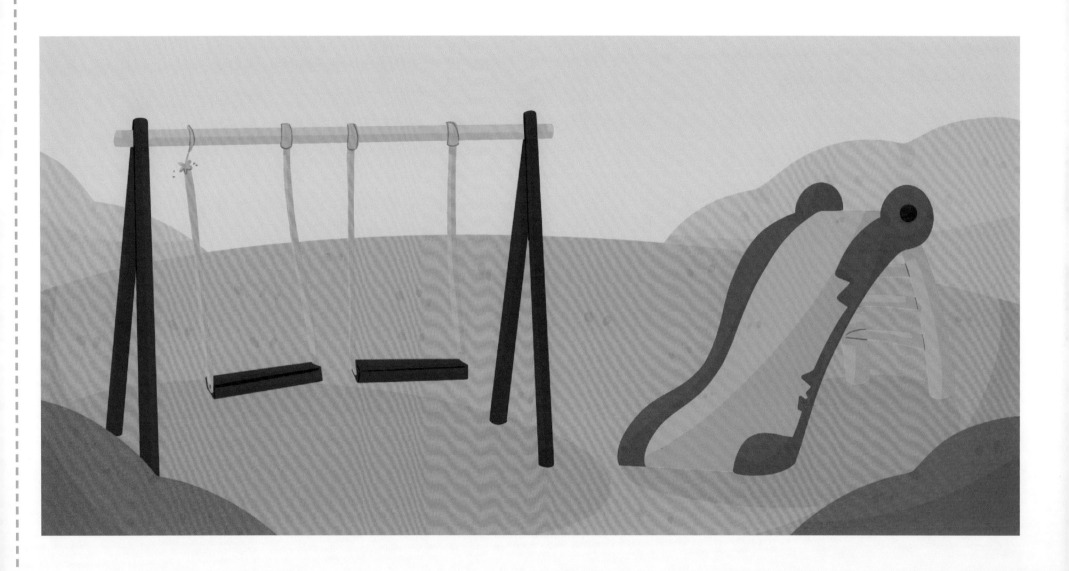

DRAWING

DRAW.

DRAW.

DRAW.

DRAW.

DRAW.

STICKERS

STICKERS

UNIT 3

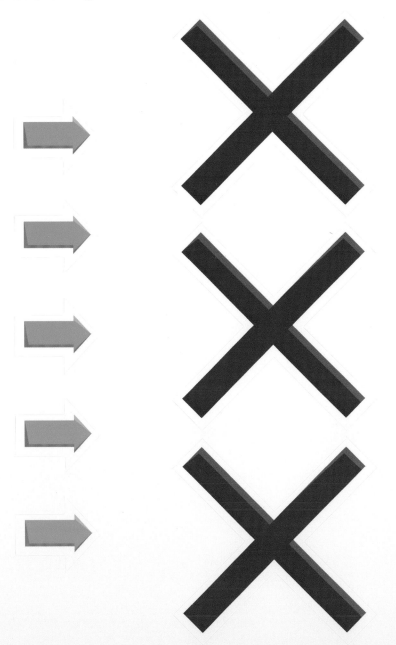

UNIT 4

STICKERS

UNIT 6

UNIT 7

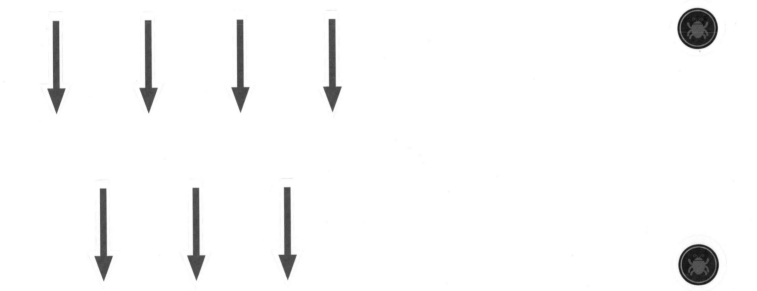